Amazing Gifts

The Story of an Exceptionally Gifted Student and a Review of Educational Acceleration

© 2014 Ronald E. Dauplaise

Disclaimer

Published by M&B Global Solutions Inc.
United States of America (USA)
ISBN: 978-1-942731-07-8

Amazing Gifts

The Story of an Exceptionally Gifted Student and a Review of Educational Acceleration

Ron Dauplaise

Contents

Preface 7

1. **(Part I)** Background 9

2. Meeting Albert 15

3. Gifted Education – Environment of the Era 19

4. The Talent Search Program 29

5. Bellin Memorial Hospital 33

6. Westinghouse Science Talent Search Program 35

7. Cray, Inc. 39

8. The Rest of the Story 43

9. **(Part II)** Comments Regarding Gifted Education 45

10. A Progressive Principal 51

11. More Is Better 57

12. Equality of Opportunity 59

13. Albert and Gifted Education – A Commentary 61

14. **(Part III)** Acceleration 63

15. Subject Matter Acceleration and Socialization 67

16. Skipping Grades 71

17. Credit By Examination 75

18. Summary 79

Acknowledgements 81

References 83

About the Author 87

Author Qualifications 88

Preface

I am going to take you through the journey of a student, "Albert," who did not graduate from high school, but went on to become one of the top software programmers in the world. You will learn how he was not identified as special in elementary school, and how and why he was missed. You may say to yourself, "How could educators *not* identify this boy as gifted?" I will answer this question by describing the thinking of educators at the time, which was from the 1970s through the 1990s. You may recognize some of these situations, as many of them continue today.

My goal is that you will gain an understanding of the challenges faced by highly gifted students, as well as their teachers and parents.

I will describe some of Albert's startling accomplishments in academic competitions in math, physics, computers and software development. At least one of those accomplishments you would not think possible. Albert's success after high school is equally as impressive as anything he had done before, as evidenced by the work he describes on his LinkedIn page.

In Part II, I will describe some school episodes with the hope that no student will have to go through what Albert did. I will also describe some successful teaching strategies in which I had occasion to observe and participate.

The last section, Part III, includes descriptions of a variety of ways to accelerate education.

Research on gifted education is plentiful. I have reviewed many sources. They are noted in the "References" section.

My thoughts on gifted education developed over forty years. I was deeply involved in gifted issues in Wisconsin for about twenty years and have followed developments from a distance for an additional eighteen while in retirement.

It has been encouraging to see the growth of interest in the gifted education field. Research has expanded. However, all in the field acknowledge there is a ways to go before all gifted students receive the services to which they are entitled.

Until all gifted students are identified and served appropriately, our country is in danger of losing a share of what could be its most critical resource: intellectual power.

Hopefully you will enjoy reading the story of Albert and learn a bit about gifted education along the way. If you are inclined, I would be most appreciative for your review on Amazon.

Ron Dauplaise

Part I - Chapter 1

Background

Identifying the gifted student has been a major challenge throughout most of American educational history. Early on, it was not uncommon for many small schools to place two or more grades in a single classroom, taught by a single teacher.

I attended such a school when I was in grades four, five and six. There were two grades per room through eighth grade. This allowed students in the lower of the two grades to be exposed to material taught to those in the grade above. This, in turn, allowed those lower-grade students to progress more rapidly if they were capable. Some in my class did, indeed, progress about two grades in one year.

As class sizes grew, it seemed more efficient to have only one grade per room, per teacher, on a regular basis. This led to a belief among the majority of educators that it would be best if all students in each classroom were on the same page, in the same book, on the same day. The thinking was this arrangement would provide students with more instructional minutes per day because teachers no longer would have to split their time between grade levels.

Little consideration was given to students who had widely varying degrees of ability. Often, teachers would try to adapt as best they could to the needs of each student, though not all teachers would address these varying learning abilities with enthusiasm. This led to widely varying levels of achievement among students, depending on which teacher a student had. Those students who learned at a slower rate often were greatly challenged or even left behind. The unfairness of this approach became apparent, eventually leading to the development and expansion of Special Education programs.

These programs allowed educators to teach each student according to that child's ability. Eventually, students were identified by use of individual psychological evaluations. A multidisciplinary team of educators and parents, commonly called an M-team, would recommend placement into one of the areas of Special Education. The M-team would create an individual education program (IEP) for each child in the program. The idea of an IEP was well-accepted by parents and educators, as it made sense with the goals of American education. Public Law 94-142 required the instatement of this IEP process nationwide.

For seventeen of my thirty-three years as an educator, I was a Special Education Supervisor specializing in Speech and Language (SES-S/L for short). Eight of my last nine years I was also a Speech-Language Pathologist (SLP), with the 1990-91 year assigned exclusively to the district's gifted program. While in these positions, I participated in several M-teams and IEP meetings.

While the IEP process met the needs of the handicapped learner, generally referring to students in the lowest 3 percent, no similar action was taken to meet the needs of students in the highest 3 percent as measured by group achievement tests. For example, if a student tested at the 99th percentile (meaning their test score was better than 99 percent of all other scores on that test), it was assumed they knew most of the material or at least would not have to work hard to master it. These students would not have a challenging experience in school. There are many stories of bored students, and it is unclear if educators were aware that some of this boredom was due to teaching below these students' capabilities.

During the 1990-91 school year, I was assigned as a Program Support Teacher-Gifted/Talented (PST-G/T) in the Green Bay (Wisconsin) Area Public Schools (GBAPS). In this position, I observed another approach beyond that of IEP. Students who were known to learn faster than their classmates were used as tutors for those who learned more slowly, an approach that has been used for many years in various districts throughout the country. The gifted student, however, did not benefit academically from tutoring slower students. Tutoring *was* seen as an appropriate education for slow learners, which is one reason it continued for many decades. Most educators had never done it any other way, and change is always difficult.

Some educators believed that tutoring would keep the fast learners from getting too far ahead and *were* helping their classmates. I believe it was true that such students did not move ahead of their classmates, but that should not be the goal of an appropriate education. Federal law emphasizes that each student must be provided a "free appropriate public education," or FAPE. This use of tutoring does not meet the "appropriate" requirement of federal law. However, FAPE had not been included in the original legislation.

Something needed to change. This and other issues motivated our Board of Education and superintendent in 1990 to create two positions of PST-G/T, one for secondary education and one for elementary.

My assignment as the PST-G/T was to work with the gifted secondary students, those in grades seven through twelve residing in Green Bay's four high schools and four junior high schools. Since I was the only PST-G/T working at this level, in the first year for this position, in a school district with about 10,000 secondary students, I certainly felt challenged! The other PST-G/T, my fine colleague Bev, worked with the kindergarten through sixth-grade students. We worked closely together.

I had been highly involved in the gifted field for roughly ten years in the GBAPS. I was already aware of programs, projects, activities and classes directed toward gifted students and had taken several courses from some of the most renowned authorities in the country. To my knowledge, no other administrator in our district had studied gifted education, and because of this, the superintendent appointed me in 1979 to coordinate gifted activities while I was the SES-S/L.

With strong support from others on our staff, Bev and I were able to replicate the Olympics of the Mind (OM) competition in Northeast Wisconsin. This national program originated in New Jersey later became Odyssey of the Mind and then Destination Imagination. It is a problem-solving and creative-thinking competition focused on student growth and development.

Furthermore, around 1985, I was able to help start the Advanced Placement (AP) program in Green Bay. Created and administered by the College Board, the AP program offers college-level curriculum and examinations to high school students. My work in this program led me to become a consultant for the College Board, and I traveled throughout northern Wisconsin for three years helping other districts initiate their own AP programs.

Since I had done extensive work in the gifted field, many teachers and administrators became aware of my activities. As the 1990-'91 school year went by, it was to my benefit that I grew to know a few hundred teachers and all the administrators in the GBAPS. One of those relationships led to my interaction with a fascinating student who had fallen through the cracks of traditional education.

Chapter 2

Meeting Albert

"Albert," the major subject of this book, was referred to me in the early fall of 1990 by a school social worker and long-time colleague. She had come across him regarding his school attendance, which was infrequent. She knew something should be done, but was not sure what.

My first try to meet Albert at his high school was not successful. He was not there. Albert attended school infrequently—about twice a week according to his own admission—and I was told that I would be lucky to catch him at school at all. I had reviewed the school social worker's records on Albert, giving me a better understanding of his attendance record and his testing history. However, a few days later I did meet him for the first time in a conference room in the Guidance Department.

Albert was about five feet, six inches or so, lean and soft-spoken. I asked him about his school attendance. In sum, he felt that since he could learn any course material in a short time – a week or two – he did not see the need to come to class except to take tests. Test-taking, I learned, was something that Albert relished. He would be willing to take a final exam without attending class. None of his teachers or the principal was willing to let him go this route.

It seems that the teachers knew enough about him that they believed he could, indeed, "ace" any course in school without being taught, even if he had a book for only a week or so. The only way a teacher would give him an A, however, was if he attended their class like all other students. In other words, he could only earn an A if a teacher taught him each day. Albert summarized his belief in a single thought, "Why should there be a special effort to customize teaching to one individual?"

When asked about homework by Milwaukee Journal reporter Jo Sandin in her April 2, 1991, article, Albert said, "If I already know it, why do it?"[29] Doing drills on material he already knew seemed a waste of time to Albert.

Albert did, however, attend class when tests were scheduled. Since he did not attend many classes, he was not awarded many A's. A few teachers, though, told me they could not in good conscience fail him, because his tests proved he knew the material, no matter what the course.

His biology teacher told me that he gave him a B, telling me he could not fail a student who got an A on each test but did not attend class regularly.

His computer teacher, a good friend of mine, told me he quickly realized that Albert knew all the material. I asked how he handled such a student. He said he assigned Albert to a computer and "let him do his own thing." The teacher would be available if needed.

Albert did not turn in any assignments for one course in particular: Consumer Education. He called this course "foolishness," and did not attend very often, even though the class was a graduation requirement. Because Albert failed this required course, he was not allowed to graduate with his class.

Academic Competition

Earlier, I had mentioned that Albert truly liked to take tests. During one of our meetings, he showed me a large clasped, manila envelope filled with several awards, many blue ribbons and medals he had earned in a variety of academic competitions. He had been recognized two consecutive years as the top mathematics student in Northeast Wisconsin, which includes tens of thousands of students. He wrote the only perfect math paper in the history of the Wisconsin State Math Meet. High school math and computer courses clearly were not a challenge for him.

Albert's most noteworthy example of test-taking achievement occurred during his junior year in the annual Wisconsin Junior Science Competition, hosted each spring at Milwaukee School of Engineering (MSOE). Each high school in the state could send one student to take a test in several science fields. At the end of the day, the exams would be scored and a convocation held, at which time the winners in each science discipline were announced. Schools would send only their best student in each discipline to take these tests. Albert's coach for this event, a math teacher and friend of mine, related this incident to me.

This teacher assembled a "team" of three boys who wanted to participate in the competition. Two were seniors, one who later went to California Institute of Technology and was elected a class officer there, while the other went to Massachusetts Institute of Technology (MIT). The third boy was Albert. The three boys decided who would take which test. Albert volunteered to take the physics test.

At the convocation, the emcee announced, "The winner of the 1990 competition in physics is Albert. Congratulations, Albert."

Competing against the best high school physics students in Wisconsin, winning was truly an outstanding achievement. Even more amazing to the other coaches was what Albert's coach said in response to the question, "How did you prepare Albert so well to win this event against such strong competition?" His answer: "Since we do not offer physics until a student is a senior, and Albert is a junior, he has not only not taken the course, but he also has not yet seen the textbook." The other coaches were in disbelief.

I asked Albert about this. How *did* he manage to earn recognition as the top physics student in Wisconsin? His reply was simple. "Mr. Dauplaise, physics is nothing but logic." All I could reply was, "Oh." I did think, though, that if physics was nothing but logic for him, it was also nothing but logic for all the rest of the top students, too. Albert was clearly the top physics student in Wisconsin.

Chapter 3

Gifted Education – Environment of the Era

While conducting background work regarding Albert for this book, I learned that similar incidents were common throughout the country.

Since Albert was not going to graduate from high school, I went back to his elementary school to try and learn how he did there. I learned an interesting fact while talking with the school's principal, another long-time acquaintance of mine. I already knew that it was not unusual to detect a prejudice against exceptionally gifted students among educators.

My conclusion may not be entirely justified, I admit, but it appears some teachers are intimidated by students who are brighter than they are, even at the elementary level. Research has confirmed my impression.

In any event, the principal informed me that, "We have never had a gifted student in my over twenty years as a principal." I explained that the definition of a gifted student in the GBAPS required, among other things, an achievement test score of at least the 97th percentile.

A single test score is not always the most valid way to identify a gifted student, but it is often a solid starting point. Albert had scored at the 99th percentile on every achievement test he had taken. Although the principal noted that may be true, Albert did not earn straight A's from his staff.

Therefore, by his definition, Albert was not gifted. This principal's definition of a gifted student was extremely narrow— only straight-A students could be gifted. End of discussion.

I had the opportunity to discuss the gifted issue with many of Green Bay's principals. One of them told me that his staff already knew all the gifted students because they were the ones who always got straight A's. He had the same definition of gifted as the other principal. I told him that one of the things we were interested in was identifying the underachieving gifted, or students who were not getting straight A's for whatever reason but had the ability to do so.

We, as a district, wanted to take steps to help them achieve their potential. I also told him this problem was not limited to the GBAPS but was prevalent throughout the country. I thought this point might make it more comfortable for him to discuss the possibility of underachieving gifted students. He simply, and politely, told me that they had never had any such student, and he had been a principal for many years.

What I had learned from these two principals confirmed that Green Bay was no different from many school districts of the era.

These two principals reinforced a saying I learned from a psychologist a few years ago: "What you are is where you were when." Translated simply, it means your thinking and actions are based on where you were at any given time.

For example, if these men were raised and educated during the Depression or World War II, then their thinking is strongly influenced by what they experienced during those times. Most likely, they were not presented with the idea of educating gifted students differently than other students while they were getting their college education. Therefore, they could not be expected to think in another way. Understanding this point made it easier for me to see where they were coming from in their thinking. Again, change is difficult.

Another relevant incident happened in the mid-1980s. As I mentioned before, I had been a SES-S/L for seventeen years, and while in this position I attended countless administrative meetings.

At one of these meetings, our superintendent divided the group of about seventy administrators, directors and supervisors among seven tables. The purpose was to brainstorm ideas our district should consider to improve our education mission; that is, providing the best education for *all* students. He directed that, as much as possible, each table should have no more than one person from each administrative category.

I was the only Special Education Supervisor (there were five in our school district) at my table, along with one high school principal, one junior high principal, and about a half-dozen other education professionals. The goal of brainstorming centers on creating as many ideas as possible and writing them *all* on a large sheet of easel paper, allowing everyone to easily see what has been suggested. *No idea is to be rejected at this time.* After discussion, the ideas are ranked at each table. Afterward, groups re-gather into one large group and review all ideas. No idea is to be rejected until everyone at the meeting has had a chance to see it.

I suggested that our district consider the needs of gifted students. After a brief discussion, I was a bit taken aback when the rest of the people at my table decided not to consider such needs. That was the end of that discussion. My suggestion was deemed unacceptable and was not written on our sheet.

The needs of the gifted student were not mentioned at any of the other tables either, leaving the topic completely ignored.

That illustrated the position of gifted education in the mid-1980s in our district. It was a challenging environment in which to work for the interests of gifted students, and it is easy to see how a student such as Albert could easily slip through. It seemed that very little was done to challenge Albert, except in math.

Expecting teachers to change, like we were proposing, was asking a great deal. Change is as difficult for teachers as it is for anyone, and altering the way a teacher approaches the teaching of gifted students is as hard as anything they will ever do. Either a teacher believes what they are doing is best and does not need to be changed, or they believe that exceptionally gifted students need nothing different than their other students. Again, change is difficult.

Think of yourself. Suppose you have been doing something one way for a long time, like driving a certain route to work, and someone tells you to change your route because there is a better way. First, you would have to concentrate on *not* going your old way. Then, you must remember the new route so you don't get lost. A teacher would go through the same type of experience trying to teach one student differently than the others in the class. Trying to use two different teaching approaches at the same time in one classroom is immensely challenging.

"Resistance to change is the tendency to reject new ideas and new ways of seeing or doing without examining them fairly…. One reason to resist change is excessive regard for tradition….Change makes us break our routine. We believe that the old way must be best because those before us did it that way." (#28, p.40)

Some teachers may decide their traditional way of teaching is best in all cases. But what exactly is tradition? It may be more like the path in the following verse:

> One day through the primeval wood
>
> A calf walked home as good calves should;
>
> But made a trail all bent askew,
>
> A crooked trail as all calves do.
>
>
> Since then three hundred years have fled,
>
> And I infer that calf is dead.
>
> But still he left behind his trail,
>
> And thereby hangs my moral tale.
>
> The trail was taken up next day
>
> By a lone dog that passed that way;
>
> And then a wise bellwether sheep
>
> Pursued the trail o'er hill and glade
>
> Through those old woods a path was made.
>
>
> And many men wound in and out
>
> And dodged and turned and bent about
>
> And uttered words of righteous wrath

Because 'twas such a crooked path;

But still they followed—do not laugh—

The first migrations of that calf,

And through this winding wood-way stalked

Because he wobbled when he walked.

This forest path became a lane

That bent and turned and turned again;

This crooked lane became a road,

Where many a poor horse with his load

Toiled on beneath the burning sun,

And traveled some three miles in one.

And thus a century and a half

They trod the footsteps of that calf.

The years passed on in swiftness fleet,

The road became a village street;

And thus, before men were aware,

A city's crowded thoroughfare.

And soon the central street was this

Of a renowned metropolis;

And men two centuries and a half

Trod in the footsteps of that calf.

Each day a hundred thousand rout

Followed this zigzag calf about

And o'er his crooked journey went

The traffic of a continent.

A hundred thousand men were led

By one calf near three centuries dead.

They followed still his crooked way,

And lost one hundred years a day;

For such reverence is lent

To well-established precedent.

A moral lesson this might teach

Were I ordained and called to preach

For men are prone to go it blind

Along the calf-path of the mind.

And work away from sun to sun

To do what other men have done.

They follow in the beaten track,

And out and in, and forth and back,

And still their devious course pursue,

To keep the path that others do.

They keep the path a sacred groove,

Along which all their lives they move;

But how the wise old wood-gods laugh,

Who saw the first primeval calf.

Ah, many things this tale might teach—

But I am not ordained to preach.

By Sam Walter Foss

"Being open to change…means being willing to suspend judgment long enough to give every new idea, no matter how strange it seems, a fair chance to prove itself." (#28, p. 41)

Some teachers *were* open to change. These teachers learned the benefit of using a different approach to teaching gifted students. An additional benefit, some teachers told me, was that they found they could use similar techniques and activities with the rest of their students, too. They learned the art of asking questions, which is a major skill in the classroom setting.

Gradual change did take place, but a school district must *continually* provide in-service programs to demonstrate the benefits of different teaching methods. A single, required in-service program for educators to discuss teaching the gifted is *definitely* not sufficient. One such program is just a start, an introduction.

For example, I learned of a school district in another state that was required to provide such an in-service. The teachers and administrators all attended, then went back and continued doing things exactly the same way they had done before. The district administrator quoted a law which appeared to prohibit starting a child in kindergarten before he was five years old. This administrator then ignored another statute that expressly allowed early entrance as long as it was approved by the local district.

The superintendent told the parents that they could start their boy in a private school and then transfer him to the public school when he reached second grade. They were told his age would not matter at that time. The boy had already completed the kindergarten curriculum, taught by a certified teacher, by age three in a preschool program and repeated it when he was four. The parents' fear, justifiably, was that he would become bored quickly and may get turned off from school. The boy's hobby was studying astronomy.

This appears to be a perfect example of a district that is incapable of change. Change is difficult. The parents did end up sending the boy to a private school and have no plans of sending him to a public school in the future.

Leadership from the top is critical. Our gifted efforts had strong support from our superintendent, which made all the difference.

Chapter 4

The Talent Search Program

While on the topic of school, Albert mentioned his experience at college while still in high school. He was allowed to enroll at the University of Wisconsin-Green Bay (UWGB) for calculus while still a senior. His enrollment in college calculus was the last step in a Green Bay program we had adopted called the Talent Search Program.

In 1981, the Board of Education accepted an idea I had read about in Smithsonian Magazine. The article discussed a study done by Dr. Julian Stanley of Johns Hopkins University, called the Study of Mathematically Precocious Youth (SMPY).[30] The SMPY was a long-term project started in 1972 whose goal was math acceleration.

Dr. Stanley, a nationally renowned leader in gifted education, identified seventh- and eighth-grade students who were talented in math. To do this, he first looked at group achievement test scores and selected those at the 97th percentile and higher. This small group of students then was given the Scholastic Aptitude Test (SAT), the nation's most widely used college entrance exam. The SAT is designed for college-bound high school students, with virtually no top score limit for seventh or eighth graders.

Dr. Stanley felt he needed such a test for this group, since achievement tests are designed for specific grades. Therefore, a student can get a maximum score on an achievement test by getting all the questions right, which many gifted students do. This means there is no way for a teacher to tell who might have been able to go further. The SAT would reveal different levels of math ability. (Achievement tests measure what you have learned, while aptitude tests measure what you might learn, especially in a specific area.)

Dr. Stanley's idea was that those who scored at least in the 97th percentile on an achievement test would reveal a range of scores on the SAT. That is, all these students would fall into various levels rather than the same level as they do on the achievement test. This identification approach did not require a teacher or administrator recommendation. The student identified themself by their test results, an objective approach strengthening the process in cases with students such as Albert, who never would have been identified if a recommendation from a teacher or administrator had been required.

After the SAT results were reviewed, Dr. Stanley selected a small number of students who scored at a certain level to take algebra in summer school. We followed Dr. Stanley's SMPY program closely, but we only looked at seventh graders in both public and private schools. Those students who scored at the 97th percentile or better on their most recent achievement test, and took the SAT and earned a high enough score, were given the opportunity to take algebra in the summer after grade seven.

Our summer algebra course was held at UWGB. It was a three-week program with fifteen days of two hours of instruction per day. We hired an algebra teacher from the Green Bay Area Public Schools to teach the course.

The students took a nationally standardized final exam at the end of the three weeks. If they passed this test, they would be enrolled in geometry in grade eight, two years earlier than most other students in our district. These students then would take advanced algebra as freshman, math analysis as sophomores; and calculus as juniors. That was as far as our math curriculum went. This is the sequence of courses Albert followed.

The GBAPS was responsible for providing an *appropriate* math course for seniors. To do this, we arranged with UWGB and St. Norbert College to enroll these students in college-level calculus. This course went faster and more in-depth than our high school course, with regular college credit awarded at its conclusion. Because of this, these students were able to earn eight college credits, which Albert did. Even though Albert could not graduate from high school due to failing the required Consumer Education course, he had a 4.0 GPA after two semesters of college calculus.

Albert said he attended the first day of the calculus course so he could learn the dates of scheduled exams. I knew almost immediately what he was going to say next. Albert relayed that he attended class only on the seven days of the exams, and that is how he earned an A. He had taught himself calculus.

The college instructor apparently was only interested in the fact that Albert had mastered the material, even if he did it in his own way. Not all college instructors would be so accepting but this one was.

Chapter 5

Bellin Memorial Hospital

After meeting Albert, it became apparent to me, as it did to the social worker, that something needed to be done soon to get Albert into a program or job where he could make productive use of his outstanding abilities. In this regard, I contacted the director of the toxicology lab at Bellin Memorial Hospital in Green Bay. I had met Dr. Dave some years earlier, and we had a good chat regarding Albert's abilities. He thought he might be able to help out Albert, and that Bellin would benefit, too.

Dr. Dave met with Albert and told him of a problem that had developed at the Bellin lab. Bellin had recently acquired a new computer, an IBM mainframe, but no one on the staff knew how to run the software. Did Albert think he could help? Albert accepted the challenge. Dr. Dave thought it may take him two weeks or so to learn the software.

The day after Albert first saw the computer, Dr. Dave stopped by to see how things were going. Albert, who was known to work twenty-four hours a day when focused on a project, told Dr. Dave that he was done! In a TV-11 interview on its "Home Town Heroes" segment (#4), Dr. Dave spoke about his surprise at the complexity of what Albert had done, "I was amazed!" he said. Albert's work was a major benefit to Bellin Hospital, as he was now prepared to teach the Bellin staff how to run their new software. This job was just the start for Albert.

Chapter 6

Westinghouse Science Talent Search Program

In October 1990, I learned of the Westinghouse Science Talent Search Program (WSTSP). The goal of the program is to provide an opportunity for high school seniors across the country to develop an original science project, write it up in detail, and submit it for judging. Historically, the WSTSP attracts about 1,500 entries each year.

Since students can enter the contest only once while in high school, the competition features primarily high school seniors. I learned that the standard procedure included starting the project in the student's junior year of high school, where the student would arrange guidance from a science teacher. The projects must be complete and the write-up sent in no later than November 30.

I thought Albert was a perfect candidate for the WSTSP. I described the program to him in detail during a meeting in October 1990, his last year in high school. He was interested and had many immediate ideas. I advised him of the time crunch. He had only about six weeks to complete his project, while other students in the WSTSP already had been working on their projects for over a year. In total, he had about seven weeks, but we had to allow time for proofreading his manuscript and for my secretary to type it.

We made arrangements to meet the following week, at which time he agreed to have narrowed his ideas down to three. At this meeting, he would commit to just one final project. However, on the scheduled decision day, Albert failed to show. When he did come to school a few days later, I asked if he narrowed his list down to three. He replied that he had. He then surprised me when he added, "I decided to do the three projects to completion."

"What?!" I thought. Albert wanted to review them with me and we would jointly decide which one to submit.

Completing three projects in just several days *and* competing against the best science students in the United States sounded beyond reasonable. We chatted a bit and quickly decided on one of the projects rather than going through all three. Albert made the final selection himself, and though I cannot remember the other two projects, I do remember the one he chose. Even though he completed the project in only a few days, I felt it had a real possibility of being one of the top projects in the country *if* he could write it up in time for my secretary to prepare it.

His project consisted of developing computer software that would allow an operator to track thirty-two objects simultaneously, no matter speed, vector or location on the globe. He entitled his project, "Simultaneous Calculations of 32 Vehicular Movements." Keep in mind this was his thinking in the fall of 1990, when personal computers – the only kind available to him – were not nearly as powerful as those on the market years later. Although I was not computer savvy, I thought his project had great potential.

What kind of computer would be able to run this software? Albert, in his to-the-point style, told me that he could not find a computer on the market that could handle his creation. For an instant, I mentally scratched the idea as too impractical for the WSTSP competition. No sooner had I thought this than Albert offered a solution almost in the same breath. Albert proposed that since he could not find a computer to run his software, he would build his own computer from scratch using off-the-shelf parts on which he had already tried his software. The idea worked. Creativity and thinking differently were clearly strong characteristics for Albert.

Since Albert now had developed both the software and hardware, and proved they worked, I stressed the urgency of his write-up. This was in an era before personal computers were common in every home, and Albert hand-wrote his presentation. He delivered his manuscript to me in late November and I immediately handed it off to my secretary, Carol. Carol immediately went to work, even though she was not used to interpreting the electrical symbols and vocabulary (neither was I). Nonetheless, Carol did a truly outstanding job. We were able to pack up everything and personally carry the entire project to UPS to get it logged in at the last possible moment. It was close!

One can imagine the judges from the WSTSP receiving about fifteen hundred sophisticated science projects that following week. The initial phase of judging was to identify the top 20 percent—roughly three hundred or so--as semi-finalists. After a second step of judging, including background on each student and various other criteria, they would select the top forty finalists, less than one student per state.

These forty individuals then would be invited to Washington, D.C. to be interviewed and demonstrate their projects. Each of the forty students would receive a substantial college scholarship. Since most of these students were seniors in the process of making final commitments to colleges, the judging was to be completed soon, before Christmas.

Shortly before Christmas break in 1990, I received a call. Carol said, "It's from Washington, D.C. I'm not sure who it is." My first thought was that the call could only concern Albert and the WSTSP. The caller told me that Albert had been selected as one of the three hundred semi-finalists, and they were now about to decide who the forty finalists would be.

It looked as if Albert was a prime candidate to be selected into this elite finalist group. My thought was how great it would be for Albert to be awarded a several thousand-dollar scholarship. However, the first question the caller asked posed a problem. "Describe Albert's high school attendance." That did it. Albert was immediately eliminated from further consideration.

I was disappointed, but oddly enough, I questioned whether Albert was as disappointed as me. At one time, Albert had told me that what he really wanted was access to a lab and left alone so he could create. He liked to work alone. My impression was that he did not think he would gain a lot by taking four years of college courses, many of which he had little interest in. He could, instead, better spend his time studying and experimenting in physics, computers and software development.

In retrospect, I agree that Albert was not the average nineteen-year-old about to enter college. In any event, as far as I know, this was the last time Albert considered college as a viable option.

Chapter 7

Cray, Inc.

Educators *cannot* let significant talent such as Albert go to waste. The problem we faced was what could be done for him now, with only about one semester left in his high school career? About this time, I remembered one of the major supercomputer designers and builders in the world, Cray, Inc., had their headquarters in Chippewa Falls, Wisconsin, about a four-hour drive west of Green Bay. Maybe Albert could fit in there, since his WSTSP project may be something they would look at.

I called Cray and talked with an executive who, among other duties, arranged assignments for college interns and students seeking work study positions. During this conversation, I detailed Albert's abilities and situation. This conversation took some time, as I felt that I was only going to have one opportunity to "sell" Albert.

The executive told me that each year they took on at least one intern from UW-Eau Claire, which was only about thirty minutes away from their headquarters. Intern positions were not permanent, but would be a great way to get Albert started in the high tech industry. We had a very extensive discussion, and afterward he agreed to review Albert's write-up and let me know one way or the other. I immediately faxed him Albert's write-up.

A day or two later, the Cray executive called. He and several other Cray principals had reviewed Albert's work. They decided they wanted to go to the next step and interview Albert. (As a point of interest, Cray produced the supercomputers for the CIA, the National Security Agency, and the Department of Defense, among others. They continue to produce for major agencies and companies around the world.)

Cray wanted a GBAPS representative to accompany Albert to the interview in Chippewa Falls. A science teacher from Albert's high school was appointed to accompany him. Since I had done much work with Albert and had made the phone contacts with Cray staff, I truly wished to accompany Albert, but it was not to be. I was not a science teacher.

A short time after the April interview, I received a call from Cray. They had decided to take a rather unusual step. Even though Albert was not enrolled in college, and probably would not be admitted to any four-year program, Cray had decided to offer Albert an internship starting in their Research Department. It sounded ideal to me, finally giving Albert a lab to work in -- one of the best in the world—while doing what he wanted to do in computer technology and software development. Albert accepted the position, starting at Cray on April 22, 1991, as a researcher, at age nineteen. I was excited for him.

Several weeks after Albert had started at Cray, I followed up. Recall that when particularly focused on a project, Albert liked to work alone, sometimes for extended lengths of time. That, however, is not the way most corporations operate. It turned out that often Albert would work long, consecutive hours, and then come in late to work the next day. As a result, when Cray needed him at a meeting, too many times he was not there. Unfortunately, Cray released him.

I was frustrated. This talent just could *not* go to waste. However, at this point, I had lost track of Albert. My position as PST-G/T was eliminated due to GBAPS budget issues, but I remained in the GBAPS district as a Speech/Language Pathologist at the elementary level. I truly enjoyed my time in this position, since we had an exceptional staff at my home school. The environment in this school fit all of us, and learning was fun and effective, as it should be for all students.

Albert's M-Team

In February 1991, I arranged for an M-team meeting to be held in Albert's high school to plan for his future. There were about a dozen educators in attendance, including the principal, guidance counselors, his social worker, school psychologist and teachers. They agreed that it was now too late for Albert to meet GBAPS graduation requirements, but they did develop a Plan B for Albert to take the GED test. The GED covers a wide variety of high school courses and would allow Albert to earn a high school equivalency diploma. The test is administered in our area at Northeast Wisconsin Technical College (NWTC). Albert agreed to take it.

Remember, Albert relished taking tests. I could foresee what the test results would be, and I think all members of his M-team knew what the results would be, too. Shortly after Albert took the test, I received a call from the NWTC test administrator, who knew I had been Albert's test facilitator. He was greatly surprised by the results, and I "innocently" asked what he meant.

Never in his several years of administering the GED had he seen such scores! Albert had scored the highest possible score on every section of the test. He got every single question correct. The test administrator wondered why such a student, one with obviously high ability, ended up taking this test. I brought him up to date.

Chapter 8

The Rest of the Story

In the spring of 2012, twenty-one years later, my curiosity was still present. Albert was now around forty years old, and one of my daughters located him on LinkedIn. On his site, he included some of his professional experiences. Living in the Greater Minneapolis-St. Paul area of Minnesota, Albert had been employed by Microsoft as a Senior Software Developer since 2009 and a Software Architect for Dow Jones Online since 2002, "helping drive a culture of excellence in the context of a large corporation by researching technology, sharing knowledge with colleagues, and leading implementation."

In his role as a Software Architect for Dow Jones, he listed as his specialties: "Software architecture. Software implementation, human interface factors, pragmatic system design, technology alternative comparison, development planning, developer training." It is clear that Albert had developed into a highly specialized computer consultant.

For me, reading this information completed the loop regarding Albert. I contacted him via his LinkedIn site. He said he remembers his Cray experience as "kick starting" his career in high tech.

Shortly after Albert was recognized as a WSTSP semifinalist, the Milwaukee Journal-Sentinel sent a reporter to Green Bay to produce a long feature article about him, including a picture. The TV news interview mentioned earlier, "Hometown Heroes," included a one-to-one interview and a picture of his WSTSP project, as well as an interview with Dr. Dave. The TV reporter ended the piece by saying, "School or no school, the future looks bright for Albert." How right he was.

Albert's LinkedIn site is broken into two categories, Dow Jones Online Media and Microsoft. As of this writing, his Dow Jones Online Media site had 444,733 followers and the Microsoft site had 376,512.

Albert asked if I had a copy of the newspaper article, as he had lost track of his some time ago. I sent him a copy.

Part II - Chapter 9

Comments Regarding Gifted Identification

When a procedure to identify gifted students starts with a teacher recommendation requirement, many underachieving gifted students will be missed. Research has shown repeatedly that teachers will miss about 50 percent of these gifted students. Albert was missed because educators looked only at his classroom performance and focused on the fact he did not get straight A's. It may be that teachers only look at straight-A students as directed by their principals. This may be what happened to Albert.

Educators need to look at more than one criterion to help them identify gifted students. Dr. Stanley used only the SAT math scores in his 1972 study because he was seeking only mathematically precocious youth. He followed his small group for a number of years, and his study remains valuable in that it illustrated how a test could identify students who were gifted in math.

I have known teachers who were mortified when some students were identified as gifted based on an achievement test when they had shown nothing outstanding in their daily work. One teacher spoke on the discrepancy, "Don't administrators trust our professional judgment?" In discussion with some teachers, I learned they had not been exposed to literature on gifted education or anything related to its identification.

A red flag for a teacher is when a student says they are bored. Boredom with school also should attract the attention of parents. It certainly is not always an indicator of giftedness, but the situation should be addressed immediately, both at school and at home. My teacher friends were basing their judgment on what they thought was giftedness--research on the topic was not involved in their training program. This may have been another incident of "what you are is where you were when."

I have discussed the difficulty in getting educators at all levels to change. Change is not impossible, but it can be extremely difficult. Some will resist change because they believe that by doing so, they are admitting that they have been wrong. Therefore, they dig in their heels as a way of signaling they will never change. These types of teachers should not be assigned to teach identified gifted students. This is an important point, because some administrators assign staff based on seniority alone.

In fact, younger teachers, those most recently trained, may be best suited to teach the gifted. Some colleges and universities require coursework in gifted education. Principals and district administrators need to carefully review the coursework their teachers took while being trained and conduct focused interviews to determine their position regarding educational opportunities for gifted.

Establishing the assessment criteria necessary to identify gifted students requires a well thought-out process. "Assessment is the umbrella term for ... systematic gathering of information on a child so that an informed decision can be made. Testing is the most standardized and technical component of assessment. The other three components ... include interviews, observations, and informal procedures." (#5, p.77)

Since hundreds of districts and many states have already gone through this process, the local committee may not have to reinvent the wheel. In fact, identification criteria already may be in place via your state's Department of Public Instruction (DPI). However, not all states have adopted a definition.

Importantly, the National Association for Gifted Children (NAGC) has created a definition for gifted students, and its extensive website provides an impressive amount of references. The NAGC's definition states, "Gifted individuals are those who demonstrate outstanding levels of aptitude or competence in one or more domains."[19]

It is my opinion that a single teacher recommendation cannot be the sole determining factor to include or exclude a student from a gifted program. This view has support from numerous examples. The Talent Search Program (TSP) uses achievement test scores as the primary criterion--no teacher recommendation requested. The student, in essence, identifies themselves by their test results.

When we ran our first TSP in the 1980-'81 school year, we found one seventh-grade boy who had earned B's and C's throughout most of elementary school, as well as early into his seventh-grade year. However, he scored at the 99th percentile on his math achievement test. Additionally, he was at the 97th percentile or better in all other areas on the achievement test.

He agreed, with his parents' approval, to take the SAT with the other TSP participants. He was one of the top scorers on the test. When I interviewed him, I asked about his grades. He told me he knew he could get all A's, but decided early on that he did not want to be different from his classmates. Instead, he chose to do B or C work.

Because his SAT scores qualified him for our three-week summer algebra course, he was offered that opportunity. The course was going to be taught by an algebra teacher from his school, but he decided not to take it. Instead, he chose to take a course also being taught at UWGB, offered to seventh grade students who had been individually tested and found to have an IQ exceeding the level required by the university. The boy had been tested by one of our school psychologists shortly before I interviewed him. He no longer remained unidentified.

The students in this class came from all over the Midwest. I came to know them quite well, as I was their teacher. I taught the class as a part of a course I was taking that summer at UWGB in gifted education. To say this class was challenging is a gross understatement! We all had fun and accomplished a great deal, as each student in my class had to select a project based on aeronautics.

When the boy started eighth grade in September, he was assigned to take algebra from the same woman who had taught our three-week summer TSP algebra class at UWGB. She clearly was the right teacher for him. During the first few days of class, she contacted the school's principal and me to recommend the boy immediately take the same standardized algebra final exam that she had given the TSP students.

We made arrangements for him to take the test at the district office building where I worked. I needed to get permission to do this from our director of secondary education, who at first was not accepting of this idea. He made it clear that we had never done anything like this before. We had a discussion, and afterward he finally agreed, but was not entirely pleased.

I administered the test to the boy. After completing the test, he had to turn in any scratch work he had done, so none of the test problems would leave the building. He gave me about a half sheet of scratch paper with only a few calculations on it. I then scored the test. He scored at the 98th percentile when compared to students who had taken a full year of algebra. In essence, he taught himself algebra while taking the test.

I followed this young man through high school to see how he developed. The staff commented that they were all talking about him, especially after his junior year math class. It seemed he got only one problem wrong in the entire course -- the only one he got wrong in his entire high school career. He eventually became an electrical engineer with a degree from the University of Wisconsin.

This boy would not have been identified as gifted if teacher recommendation was the first and only criterion used for identification. In this way, he was just like Albert.

Chapter 10

A Progressive Principal

I found one principal in Green Bay who, upon looking back to the 1981-82 school year, was way ahead of her time. This woman was a nun, Sr. Juliana Dischler, O.P., the principal of a private school with grades one through eight. The only criterion to attend this school was that the family had to be a member of the parish. In other words, it was not selective.

It so happened that when a certain class of students was in the primary grades, she and her staff recognized significant differences in the abilities of the students, much more than normally would be expected. As this group of about forty children entered grade six in the fall of 1979, she decided to group them according to proven ability based on their five years of experience and achievement test scores. The class always had filled two rooms with two teachers, only now the students would not be randomly assigned. Bear in mind that grouping students was not well accepted by many educators at that time.

In one room, she assigned students she described as average learners. In the other room, she assigned students who were clearly high achieving, or gifted. Sr. Juliana knew this was a most unusual situation; indeed, she may never have a situation like this again. She told me she felt obligated to provide appropriate opportunity to *all* of the forty students, and grouping would be the best way to do it. The teaching staff also felt it was the best way to go.

When these students were in grade seven, three of the girls were in our Talent Search Program. All three took our summer algebra course, and one of the girls also took our summer writing course. This summer writing course was an example of an enrichment program, not acceleration like math.

At that time, in 1981, the SAT resulted in three scores – math, verbal, and the Test of Standard Written English (TSWE). The math and verbal scores were reported on a scale of 200 to 800, with 500 being the mean. The TSWE, however, had a maximum score of 60. One of the girls, who was only eleven years, ten months old, scored a perfect 60 on the TSWE. Needless to say, this was exceptional.

The other two girls, twelve-year-old identical twins, scored about 55, which is far above average even for high school students. I believe these outstanding results stand as testimony to an outstanding English teacher, as the TSWE tests skills that are taught, not skills that can be reasoned out like math.

I was able to follow some of these students through their high school years. This class of nineteen students continued to have academic success. Five of them became National Merit Semifinalists; three of these went on to become National Merit Finalists, including the twins. It truly was a most exceptional class. These statistics compare favorably with many selective schools. I believe it was Sr. Juliana's aggressive approach to grouping that made the significant difference. Obviously, Sr. Juliana was special, as were the teachers who showed this strategy *can* be effective. They were all comfortable with change. Tradition was not a hindrance.

• • •

I had a discussion with Sr. Juliana about the need to provide math at an appropriate level for the three girls. She knew she needed to provide math at the appropriate level for two of those TSP girls, the twins, who took algebra in the summer, and we discussed how to go about doing that. The eleven-year-old decided, with her parents' agreement, to take regular eighth grade math at the private school, the highest level of math offered there.

One of the twins who took summer algebra did not feel comfortable moving on to the next level of math, geometry, but did want to take algebra. In discussion with her later, I learned that she had not mastered the quadratic equation in the summer program. After a short time in the regular algebra class, she said she finally "got it," but by that time, unfortunately, it was too late for her to start geometry. Later, she admitted that the rest of that year was boring (there is that red flag again), as she had already learned all the material.

Sr. Juliana was confident that this girl would do *really* well in a full year of algebra. I arranged, with the full cooperation of Sr. Juliana, to schedule this girl for second hour algebra, the earliest it was offered, in the public junior high school less than a mile away. That school started at 7:30 a.m. and ran fifty-minute classes, with five minutes between each class. This meant that second period started at 8:25 and ended at 9:15. Sr. Juliana adjusted her schedule so the girl had time to get back to the private school in time for the rest of the school day and not miss any regular class time. It was a neat arrangement and an outstanding example of creative problem solving.

Sr. Juliana had the same situation with the other twin, who passed the algebra final exam. This second girl now was ready for geometry. Because geometry was not offered in grade nine at the junior high at that time, she could not go there with her sister. In this case, I worked with Sr. Juliana and the high school's principal, where geometry was offered. That principal was resistant to the idea of having a student in grade eight attend his school, which had students starting in grade ten. Not only had this never been done before, but he was concerned that there would be a social issue with such a wide age difference.

His resistance, however, was passive compared to that displayed by the district's executive director of secondary education, who was strongly opposed to this arrangement. Sr. Juliana was looking to help provide an appropriate math level for the girl, but I did most of the negotiating with him.

The executive director felt that since the girls were enrolled in a private school, they could not simultaneously attend a public school. When he expressed his strong belief that the girl going to the high school would face major social issues by attending first hour geometry, he asked her father to write a letter.

The administrator would not go along with the arrangement unless the parents took full responsibility for the girl's social welfare. The parents pointed out that the family paid taxes supporting the public schools. The father wrote the letter, and the director finally relented. The girl enrolled at the public high school for geometry, though he was quite unhappy about the situation.

Finally, arrangements were completed. The high school was a few blocks closer than the junior high, so timing for the girls would not be a problem.

Both girls got an A.

There were four other TSP math accelerated students, two of whom attended private schools. I did not hear of any notable issues with any of them enrolling for geometry in another building.

In the 1985-86 school year, I learned of an American History teacher who was a classic model of how to address the needs of some of his students. These were students whom he recognized as needing something more. "Mr. R" regularly gave reading assignments and homework so the students could demonstrate they had learned the material. It was a traditional approach.

However, for a small group of high-achieving students – they were not called gifted at that time – he wanted to present a challenge. A typical assignment required these students to write an essay explaining why they thought certain incidents occurred and what the motivation of the historical figures might have been, along with other challenging questions. These students would earn an A, but were not given the same kind of multiple choice and short answer questions on tests as the rest of the class. They had to do research beyond the textbook in order to justify their position.

In this way, Mr. R encouraged these advanced learners to develop critical thinking skills and not reply in a yes or no manner. Mr. R was successful in helping these students learn how to learn. He was a special teacher who knew how to differentiate instruction to meet the needs of students.

I interviewed some of Mr. R's students. They did not feel picked on. Rather, they accepted the challenge, as history for them was an intellectual challenge adding to school's fun. Additionally, they were learning good study habits.

Chapter 11

More Is Better

This is a story about a high school boy from a nearby district that concerns the idea that more is better.

This student could learn any subject quickly. It was clear to his parents that he needed class work that moved quickly and challenged his ability to think creatively and problem-solve. He did not need repetition to learn; rather, he sought depth. When extensive repetition was assigned, which was often, he would quite quickly become bored. He was constantly ready to move on.

What this boy experienced was the opposite of what he needed. Too many of his teachers believed the best way to keep him busy was to give him more of the same. This repetition turned him off to school. He felt it was unfair that he was required to do more than his classmates just because he could do the work quickly. He was aware of being treated differently.

Some teachers fall into this trap. It could be that it is their way of keeping all the students on the same page, on the same day. Obviously, this was an ineffective way to meet the needs of a student like this. The approach was not appropriate.

I have detailed these scenarios to illustrate the variety of situations that parents and educators can experience with the gifted. It is not easy to create change. As I have mentioned many times, change is difficult, and sometimes it is not allowed to happen at all. However, in some states there are statutes that make changes much easier, as they are mandated.

Chapter 12

Equality of Opportunity

On the surface, having all students on the same page, in the same book, on the same day seems like the fair thing to do. All students appear to be treated equally. However, since there are many different styles and rates of learning, teachers must be trained and when to make a change from this traditional approach.

While researching this topic, I found a statement that I believe sums up the issue best. The following statement was made by Mary F. Berry, Assistant Secretary for Education, U.S. Dept. of Education, May 17, 1978.

"We are committed to making equal the opportunity children have to gain an education. This is a simple concept, but it is not a simple-minded one. Equal opportunity does *not* mean exactly equal treatment for each and every student, regardless of background or condition. It *does* mean guaranteeing that every young person has an equal chance to get the kind of education that will help that individual realize his or her potential.

"There is, among too many people in this country, an unfortunate confusion between the concept of democracy and the concept of uniformity. Treating every child exactly like every other may seem democratic, but it actually is as unegalitarian (unequal) as anything could be, because it ratifies and enforces inequalities that already exist.

Giving special support to the disadvantaged or the handicapped, or to the gifted, may seem biased or elitist, but it actually enhances the democratic quality of our schools, because it makes it possible for *all* children to achieve an education that equally meets their needs. There is no conflict between special programs for special need groups and our national goal of equity in the school process. The two propositions are compatible and complementary."[2]

Chapter 13

Albert and Gifted Education
A Commentary

Albert's achievements certainly vindicate the decision our board of education and superintendent made in creating the position of PST-G/T, which allowed me to help Albert along in his field. Albert's story is a classic example of how vital it is to identify gifted students *and* provide them appropriate educational opportunities.

The story of Albert's educational experience is just one story by one educator who worked full-time for just one year in the field. In a district the size of Green Bay, it would be surprising if Albert were the only unidentified gifted student who was bored with regular class work. Admittedly, Albert's extremely high level of ability occurs very seldom. Indeed, I may never have found another like him even if my position had not been eliminated. The fact remains, however, that there are other bored gifted students out there.

Educators everywhere must be ever alert to identify gifted students and take meaningful action to provide appropriate opportunities for them to grow. Extending this issue throughout our country, one can only imagine the number of students who finish high school -- or do not finish high school -- and are unfulfilled. Research has found that the most important teacher a child has is their first grade teacher, as giftedness often can be identified at this age. Nevertheless, educators at all levels must be alert for giftedness in any area, just as they are for other special needs students.

From my observation, no public high school is designed to meet the needs of a student like Albert. But, many strategies and programs have been developed that can help all teachers provide appropriate opportunities to students like him. Educators must be open to change or it will not happen.

PART III - Chapter 14

Acceleration

Here is what the research says about acceleration:

In a study of high-ability children who had been accelerated, 71 percent reported satisfaction with their acceleration experience. Of the participants who reported they were unsatisfied, the majority indicated they would have preferred more acceleration.[16]

Talented students from accelerated classes outperform non-accelerates of the same age and IQ by almost one full year on achievement tests.[16]

Talented students from enriched classes outperform initially equivalent students from conventional classes by four to five months on grade equivalent scales.[16]

Students who were allowed early entrance to elementary school averaged six months ahead in achievement when compared to their age peers during the same year. Additionally, these students showed improvement in socialization and self-esteem compared to slight difficulties faced by advanced students who were not accelerated.[27]

A long-term study of the Academic Talent Search program demonstrated that five years beyond their participation in the program, students viewed the experience positively, attributing feelings of improved self-esteem and self-control to the program.[32]

Early Entrance

I use the term early entrance to define those students allowed to begin kindergarten or first grade ahead of peers their equivalent age. Earlier in this book, I described a situation where a boy was not admitted to grade one because his birthday did not fall before September 1.

Recall that the boy already had completed kindergarten by age three and again at age four while in a pre-school program taught by a certified teacher. The boy's home school district superintendent quoted, and interpreted, part of the state statutes that appeared to prohibit her from permitting the boy to start grade one. He was about ten weeks too young, by her interpretation.

The statutes did not say that a child could not start kindergarten before age five. The statutes specifically do say that children who were five years old by September 1 could start school. Elsewhere in the statutes, it stated that the local school district could decide by itself if a child could start kindergarten before age five or grade one before age six.

The superintendent did not tell this last bit to the parents, but the parents' lawyer did. In fact, the statutes specifically state that a local district may accept a student who was identified as gifted and had been accelerated elsewhere in the state, just as the boy had. The superintendent was clearly using a form of age discrimination.

The parents decided they did not want to send the boy to a district that clearly did not want him. If the superintendent did not want him and the teachers were not trained to teach gifted, then they were concerned there would be a negative approach to their boy in school. The literature is replete with stories of this kind of treatment happening. The parents enrolled the boy in a private school with no intention of returning to that public school district in the future.

Many states, as well as local districts, have in place a procedure to guide decision-makers regarding early entrance to school. Parents need to check on this before approaching district officials about early entrance.

Chapter 15

Subject Matter Acceleration and Socialization

The Talent Search Program is a classic example of subject matter acceleration, a strategy that involves completing coursework faster than normal. This, in turn, may allow a student to earn more credits sooner, thereby possibly graduating from high school early. Courses that lend themselves to acceleration are physics, computer programming and other sciences. This approach is ideal for gifted students like Albert.

A major concern when considering early entrance, or any grade or subject matter acceleration, centers on socialization issues. Those in control often firmly believe that a student will not "fit in" with their new classmates, most of whom are about one year older. Study after study throughout the years has shown this is not the case. However, many decision-makers have not used this research, instead basing their decision against acceleration only on feelings or what they think might happen.

In some cases, the research may be ignored, while in other cases they are not aware that research exists. One principal, after I had briefly described Albert to her, said, "He is a savant." She said she assumed that because I had mentioned that Albert liked to work alone, he must be a savant. I am not sure if she had done much study of gifted education issues.

In the summer and fall 1996 issue of the journal, "Highly Gifted Children," Kathi Kearney authored an article entitled, "Highly Gifted Children in Full Inclusion Classrooms."[15] She provides a description of the socialization issue with clarity, as follows:

"Teachers are often concerned about the play behavior of extremely gifted children, sometimes mistaking solitary play for social immaturity. It is important to understand that highly gifted children are often loners on the playground not because they lack play knowledge or are unsociable creatures, but because their advanced intellectual development causes them to 'organize the play into a complicated pattern, with some remote and definite climax as the goal' and to use vocabulary not yet accessible to age peers." (#11, p. 274)

Developmentally, their cognitive abilities already may be where neither their own motor skills nor their age-mates' minds can yet go. In inclusive classrooms, how much should such a child be encouraged or even compelled to play with age peers? Each case is different, but among children in the very highest ranges of intelligence, Hollingworth (#11, p. 275) states:

"These young children of extremely high intellectual acumen fail to be interested in 'child's play' for the same reasons that in adulthood they will fail to patronize custard-pie movies or chute-the-chutes at amusement parks. It is futile, and probably wholly unsound psychologically, to strive to interest the child above 170 IQ in ring-around-the-rosy or blind-man's buff.

Many well-meaning persons speak of such efforts as "socializing the child," but it is probably not in this way that the very gifted can be socialized. The problem of how the play interests of these children can be realized is one that will depend largely on individual circumstances for solution. Often it can be solved only by the development of solitary play."

Another piece from the NAGC website offers the following:

"Myth: Acceleration Placement Options Are Socially Harmful For Gifted Students"

"Many gifted students are uncomfortable with children their same age and are often happier learning and interacting with older children and adults. Acceleration can place advanced students with others of similar ability, reducing anxiety and abnormal behavior. Acceleration is not the answer for every gifted child, but it is a valuable option for many. According to James A. Kulik of the University of Michigan, 'Meta-analytic reviews [these are reviews of many research studies on the same topic] have consistently concluded that educational acceleration helps students academically without shortchanging them socially and emotionally."[17]

For more information about the success of acceleration, see Fiedler, et al[7], and Kulik[17] in the references.

These paragraphs clearly point out that each child's social interaction must be looked at separately. There is not one solution that fits all.

The most famous proponent of subject matter acceleration is Dr. Julian Stanley, the Johns Hopkins professor mentioned previously who did the Study of Mathematically Precocious Youth in 1972. You may remember that he was trying to identify seventh and eighth graders for math acceleration.

In 1977, Dr. Stanley concluded, "It appears that not a single substantial study has ever shown acceleration to be harmful to the typical accelerant who is intellectually able enough to warrant the use of such procedures. On the average, the results are decidedly beneficial, whereas the withholding of acceleration from able well-motivated youths is likely to harm their academic, social and emotional development. Most of the evidence against acceleration is of the 'I knew a student…' variety."[30]

The vast majority of studies show that not only do accelerated students have healthy social and emotional development, but gifted children who are *not* accelerated may also be socially less mature and emotionally more frustrated because of being kept in lock-step grades.

Being kept in lock-step grades, in turn, can lead to boredom. Boredom, as noted earlier, is one of the red flags for parents and teachers. Boredom and lack of acceleration are related.

Parents, be on the alert.

Chapter 16

Skipping Grades

Skipping grades is entirely different than early entrance. With early entrance to kindergarten, a student would not miss any grades if no other acceleration were to take place. When a student skips a grade, such as going from grade two directly to grade four, an entire grade is missed. In this situation, the student must be carefully observed, as well as evaluated. The student will finish high school at least one year sooner than students of the same age in either case.

In consolidating grades, a student will start the school year in one grade, for example grade two, and part way through the school year move into the next grade, in this case grade three. I observed this situation in action, where it seemed to be effective.

The boy I witnessed entered kindergarten reading at a high level, as many gifted students do. He was reading sports magazines and newspapers before he was four years old. The kindergarten teacher knew immediately that her pre-reading activities were boring him. With the approval of the parents, as well as the school principal, the boy went to grade one for reading lessons. As it turned out, he was past that reading level, too, but finished the year in grade one reading.

When he left the kindergarten room each day, he would arrive in the grade one room about fifteen minutes before reading time. While he waited for reading to begin, he listened to the last fifteen minutes of the grade one math class. Somewhat predictably, he absorbed much of the grade one math while he still was enrolled in kindergarten. At the end of the school year, the parents enrolled him in a private school to start grade one.

The private school immediately placed him in grade two for reading. Again, the reading time did not exactly match up, so the boy waited awhile for grade two reading to begin. While waiting, he now listened to grade two math lessons. He did this for the entirety of the year.

Grade two started out the same way as the previous two years. However, early in this school year, the principal and the teachers recommended to the parents that the boy be evaluated by the public school psychologist. The parents immediately agreed.

For some time, the boy's mother had noticed that he did not want to go to school. He would complain of a headache or stomach ache or some other mysterious ailment. In retrospect, he likely was bored and this was his way of avoiding the schoolroom.

Reportedly, what really got the mother's attention was one specific incident. The boy got up one morning and did not complain of anything. He seemed eager to go to school. When she asked him why, he said he felt good because there was going to be a spell-down and he knew he could win. As it turns out, he did not have to learn much about spelling, and he did end up winning. He was one of those students who many have heard about: he inherently knew how to spell every word at that level--and many levels beyond that as well.

After the psychological evaluation was completed, a conference was held with the parents, two teachers, principal and psychologist. The psychologist recommended that the boy join his grade three classmates full-time. All were in agreement and socialization was not seen as a problem. As the psychologist pointed out, the boy had already been in class with these students for several hours per day for one full school year, as well as the first quarter of the current school year. All in the class knew each other and played with each other on the playground. The whole environment helped create a smooth transition.

By the end of the school year, the boy had attended grade two for one quarter and grade three for three quarters. He had consolidated two school years into one.

I have detailed this boy's story to provide an example of how educators and parents can successfully work together for the academic benefit of the child.

Chapter 17

Credit By Examination

Credit by examination allows a student to take an examination to demonstrate they know the subject matter. This is what Albert asked to do, but was rejected. Moving in this direction requires firm groundwork in place with local school officials, possibly including formal policy from the school board. It may be that the state will have this approach noted clearly in the statutes. This strategy can be controversial.

When reviewing any statutes, the parents must be particularly aware of the use of the word "may." If the statute says the local district *may* permit credit by exam, it also means that the district *may not* give credit. In this case, the state intends to let the final decision up to the local district. Therefore, credit by exam could vary within the state.

Credit by exam is a strategy offered by many colleges, too. As students prepare for college, it may be in their interest to make an early inquiry about this. The common name for this process is the College Level Examination Program–(CLEP). CLEP also is commonly used by adults returning to college later in life. Students can save a substantial amount of money by reducing the amount of time required to earn a degree.

Advanced Placement

The College Board administers Advanced Placement classes, universally referred to as AP. It is the same company that administers the SAT. The SAT is also the test that Dr. Stanley used in his SMPY, and we in Green Bay used it in our Talent Search Program.

AP courses are full-year courses taught in the high schools. There are many courses available, but not every high school will offer them all. Each course is intended to cover a regular college freshman-level course. A student, therefore, can earn college credit without having to leave the high school building.

At the end of the school year, usually starting in May, the College Board designates a date for a nationally standardized final exam in each course. No more than two such exams are scheduled for the same day. All schools in the country give the same final exam on the same day. The scores are reported on a 1-to-5 scale, with most scores of 3 to 5 accepted at colleges for credit. Colleges do not all accept AP scores equally. It is best if the student checks with each potential college to determine if AP courses are accepted. The student needs to be aware of the actual numeric score each college will accept.

A student may be able to take an AP course even before their senior year in high school. It is of benefit to learn about AP before enrolling in high school as a freshman to begin planning well ahead of time. There is a fee for each test, but if a student can complete several AP courses, significant dollars and time can be saved at the college level. Many students nationwide take advantage of this cost-effective way to earn college credit.

• • •

Early Admission to College

Early admission to college is determined by each institution. Most colleges will require that a student graduate from high school before enrolling. As I noted in the AP discussion, students may earn college credits while still in high school, as well as by special examination.

A combination of these strategies will allow a student to reduce the amount of time in college, thereby reducing total college cost without necessarily requiring early admission to college. The student must research the requirements for early entry at each potential college well ahead of time.

Chapter 18

Summary

In this book, I have discussed the concept of educational acceleration in some of its many forms.

Starting with the story a single exceptionally gifted high school boy, Albert, and going on to shorter anecdotes about other students, I covered a variety of school situations. My intent was to present illustrations of a variety of situations that parents and their children may experience. Additionally, I described different ways that acceleration can be addressed.

Another intention was to describe situations for educators to gain some insight into the problems that gifted students experience. Hopefully, educators can help eliminate or avoid these problems.

I also included a discussion of acceleration and its effect on students, both academically and socially. This is a very broad topic about which there is much research. Educators should make an effort to review the research, and in this way avoid serious errors. Decisions regarding acceleration are always difficult, but by consulting the extensive research, decision-makers improve the chances of making informed choices.

There are two excellent sources to start doing your own research on the topic of gifted education. One is the website of the National Association for Gifted

Children (NAGC), which has an imposing amount of information. Another is a book entitled, "A Nation Deceived: How Schools Hold Back America's Brightest Students – Vol. II"[5]. This outstanding reference reviews most of the pertinent research that has been done, covering a wide variety of gifted topics.

Thank you for reading my book, and I would be most appreciative for your review on Amazon.

Best wishes for a successful educational journey.

Acknowledgements

I want to express a sincere thank you to several people. Without their contributions and encouragement through the years, much of what I have noted in this book would not have been possible.

Former Green Bay Public Schools superintendent Dr. Timothy Quinn, who appointed me in 1979 to coordinate the gifted effort in our school district. Without his strong leadership, the gifted initiative would not be where it is today. Our School Board, which authorized the position of Program Support Teacher – G/T, played a major role in changing the climate for gifted students. Craig Hitchens, director of curriculum, under whom I worked and who provided many suggestions and much day-to-day input, was instrumental in all gifted efforts. Craig was the first person who suggested I write about Albert more than twenty years ago. (Finally did it, Craig.)

Gini Mitchell, my immediate supervisor, who always supported me with advice and encouragement. Bev Splitgerber, the PST-G/T who worked with the elementary-level students while I worked with the secondary students. We worked closely together and shared many ideas. Carol Lambert, our secretary, who did great service for the three of us in the Gifted Department. Carol did yeoman's work to prepare Albert's WSTSP project write-up. You are deeply appreciated, Carol. Delores Delvaux was my secretary when I served as G/T coordinator, and we worked as a team. Thank you for your support, Delores. After Delores retired, Pat Brunner became my secretary and contributed her organizational talents. Thank you, Pat.

There are many other teachers and parents who influenced and helped immeasurably along my journey. A special thanks, too, to the NEWTAG Association. This large group, comprised mostly of parents but including many teachers, was critical to getting the ball rolling to the benefit of gifted children in this part of Wisconsin.

A very special thank you to my son, Mike, a professional writer, who used his nearly 35 years of experience to guide me through the entire writing process, from conception to completion. It is special when your son is your teacher. For anyone who is considering writing or publishing a book, Mike is THE guy to go to. Look him up at www.mikedauplaise.com.

A most sincere thank you to my wife, Ellen, who listened patiently to me as I worked my way along. No one has ever had a better listener. She is also a most valuable proofreader. Thank you so very much, my wife.

Ron Dauplaise
Green Bay, Wisconsin (USA)
January 2014

References

1. Bar-Lev, Nissan B. "A Revolution in Public Education Sweeping the Nation." *Green Bay Press-Gazette*, August 2013.
2. Berry, Mary F. *Assistant Secretary for Education, U.S Department of Education* (May 17, 1978).
3. Bishop, William E. "Successful Teachers of the Gifted." *Exceptional Children* (Council for Exceptional Children), January 1968: 317-325.
4. Albert, interview by Dr. Dave. *Home Town Heroes* WLUK-Channel 11, Green Bay, April 1991.
5. N. Colangelo, S.G Assouline, M.U.M Gross. *A Nation Deceived: How Schools Hold Back America's Brightest Students.* Vol. II. Iowa City, Iowa, 2004.
6. Council for Exceptional Children. *Council for Exceptional Children: The Voice and Vision of Special Education.* 2014. www.cec.sped.org.
7. E.D Fiedler, R.E Lange, S. Winebrenner. "In Search of Reality: Unraveling the Myths About Tracking, Ability Grouping, and the Gifted." *Roeper Review*, no. 16: 4-7.
8. Gardner, Howard. "Frames of Mind: The Theory of Multiple Intelligences." Harvard University, 1983.
9. Haier, R.J. *The Intelligent Brain--Course Guidebook.* Cantilly, VA: The Teaching Co., 2013.
10. Halvorson, Heidi G. "The Trouble with Bright Girls." In *The Science of Success: How We All Achieve Our Goals*, by Heidi G. Halvorson. National Association of Gifted Children, 2011.
11. Hollingworth, L.S. *Children Above 180 IQ.* Yonkers, NY: World Book Company, 1942.
12. Harnadek, Anita. *Critical Thinking, Book 2.* Pacific Grove, CA: Midwest Publications Co., 1980.
13. Hunkins, Francis P. *Teaching Thinking Through Effective Questioning.* Norwood, MA: Christopher-Gordon Publishers, Inc., 1989.

14. Juliana Dischler, Sr., O.P, interview by Ron Dauplaise. *Personal Interview* (2012).

15. Kearney, Kathi. "Highly Gifted Children in Full Inclusion Classrooms." *Highly Gifted Children* (Hollingworth) 12, no. 4 (Summer/Fall 1996).

16. Kulik, J.A. *An Analysis of the Research on Ability Grouping: Historical and Contemporary Perspectives.* University of Connecticut, Storrs: National Research Center on the Gifted and Talented, 1992.

17. J.A Kulik, N.C Angelo, S.G Assouline, and M.U Gross. *A Nation Deceived: How Schools Hold Back America's Brightest Students, VOL. II.* University of Iowa, Iowa City: University of Iowa, 2004, 13-22.

18. D. Lubinski, R.M Webb, M.J Morelock, and C. Benbow. "Top 1 in 10,000: A 10-Year Follow-Up of the Profoundly Gifted." *Journal of Applied Psychology* 86, no. 4 (2001): 720.

19. *Acceleration: What the Research Says.* 2013. www.nagc.org/index.aspx?id=3410.

20. *Myth: Acceleration Placement Options Are Socially Harmful for Gifted Students.* 2013. www.nagc.org/index2.aspx?id=5072.

21. *Pre-K Grade-12 Gifted Education Programming Standards .* 2013. www.nagc.org/index.aspx?id=546.

22. *Teacher Preparation and Program/Services Standards.* 2013. www.nagc.org/GiftedEducationStandards.aspx

23. Novella, Steven. *Your Deceptive Mind: A Scientific Guide to Critical Thinking Skills, Course Guidebook.* Chantilly , VA: The Teaching Co., 2012.

24. Page, Scott E. *The Hidden Factor: Why Thinking Differently is Your Greatest Asset, Course Guidebook.* Chantilly, VA: The Teaching Co. , 2012.

25. Renzulli, Joseph. CompassLearning. 2013. www.renzullilearning.com.

26. Renzulli, J.S., and Reis, S.M. "The Reform Movement and the Quiet Crisis in Gifted Education." *Gifted Children Quarterly* 35, no. 1 (1991): 26-35.

27. Rogers, K.B. *Re-Forming Gifted Education: How Parents and Teachers Can Match the Progams to the Child.* Scottsdale, AZ: Great Potential Press, 2002.

28. Ruggiero, Vincent R. *The Art of Thinking-2nd Edition: A Guide to Critical and Creative Thought.* New York City, NY: Harper and Rowe Publishers, 1988.

29. Sandin, Jo. *Milwaukee Journal Sentinal,* April 1991.

30. Stanley, Julian C. "A Study of Mathematically Precocious Youth." Johns Hopkins University, 1977.

31. Stevens, Scott P. *Games People Play: Game Theory In Life, Business, and Beyond, Course Guidebook.* Chantilly, VA: The Teaching Co., 2008.

32. Thomas, T.A. *Acceleration for the Academically Talented.* Eric Documents Reproduction Service, 1980.

33. U.S Department of Education. *National Excellence: A Case for Developing America's Talent.* Office of Educational Research and Improvement, Washington D.C.: Government Printing Office, 1993.

34. Universal Design for Learning (UDL). http://www.udlcenter.org.

About the Author

Ron Dauplaise is a retired educator and
public school administrator who lives just
outside of Green Bay, Wisconsin (USA).
He and his wife, Ellen, enjoy living on the
east shore of the bay of Green Bay, where
they can take in the sunsets and appreciate
the beauty of nature. Ron and Ellen have
four children and five grandchildren.

Ron keeps himself busy in retirement with a variety of interests,
including a special talent in Swiss-style chip carving. You can see his
unique carved crosses at http://carvedcrosses.com/.

When he's not busy working on wood projects, you can find Ron
giving tours at Lambeau Field, home of the Green Bay Packers. The
Dauplaise family has been season ticket holders since 1965, and Ron is
one of the leading historians of the tour guide staff.

Author Qualifications

Ronald E. Dauplaise

- B.S. Degree, Economics/Finance, University of Wisconsin-Oshkosh
- Communicative Disorders, Post-bachelors undergraduate major, UW-Eau Claire
- M.S. Degree, Communicative Disorders/Audiology, UW-Stevens Point
- U.S. Army Finance Corps, 2 years, Fort Bragg, NC
- Finance Dept., Moore Business Forms (large international printing company), 2 years.
- Special Education Supervision – Level A Certification, UW-Madison
- Gifted Education, Post-masters course work, UW-Madison, UW-Green Bay. Special professors Dr. John Feldhusen, Dr. Don Treffinger. Additional workshop: Dr. Joseph Renzulli
- Taught class of identified gifted seventh-grade students in summer session, UW-Green Bay
- Speech/Language Pathologist, 13 years, Green Bay Area Public Schools (All grade levels)
- Speech/Language Pathologist, 2 years, Lena (Wis.) Public Schools (All grade levels)
- Special Education Supervisor, Speech/Language, 17 years, Green Bay Area Public Schools
- Gifted/Talented Program Support Teacher--Secondary, 1 year, Green Bay Area Public Schools
- Coordinator of Gifted/Talented, 11 years, Green Bay Area Public Schools
- Green Bay Public Schools Teacher of the Year, one of three honored teachers in 1991-92
- Nominated for Wisconsin Teacher of the Year, 1992
- Executive Committee, Wisconsin Speech/Language Hearing Association (WSHA), 3 years
- WSHA State Convention Chair, 1 year
- Northeast Wisconsin Talented and Gifted Association (NEWTAG), Board of Directors
- Initiated Talent Search Program (TSP) in the Green Bay Area Public Schools, 1980

● ● ●

- Initiated Super Saturday Program in the Green Bay Area Public Schools, 1979
- Administrator, Advanced Placement tests, 3 years
- Administrator, SAT, 3 years
- College Board Consultant-AP, 3 years
- Consultant for College Board to help initiate AP program in six school districts
- Committee to originate Olympics of the Mind Program in Green Bay and surrounding area
- Olympics of the Mind, Wisconsin State Board of Governors
- Olympics of the Mind, Chair, First Wisconsin State Championships
- Olympics of the Mind, Coach, Fort Howard Elementary School, Green Bay
- Presenter on Gifted/Talented, Northeast Wisconsin Private Schools Spring Convention
- In-Service Presenter on Gifted/Talented, Green Bay Area Public Schools
- Current: Lambeau Field Tour Guide, Green Bay Packers, 14 years

Made in the USA
Las Vegas, NV
12 February 2022

43782364R00056